Greyfriars Bobby
The Real Story at Last

BY THE SAME AUTHOR

Scots Proverbs and Rhymes	Moray Press	(1948)
Doric Spice	Blackford Press	(1956)
The Gowks of Mowdieknowes	The Pinetree Press	(1963)
What is Education in Scotland ?	Akros Publications	(1970)
Macgregor's Mixture	Gordon Wright Publishing	(1976)
Clan Gregor	The Clan Gregor Society	(1977)
Four Gates of Lothian (Poems)	Forbes Macgregor	(1979)
Greyfriars Bobby	The Ampersand	(1980)
Authenticated Facts Relating to Greyfriars Bobby	Forbes Macgregor	(1980)
Salt-sprayed Burgh	The Pinetree Press	(1981)
More Macgregor's Mixture	Gordon Wright Publishing	(1983)
Famous Scots	Gordon Wright Publishing	(1984)
Scots Proverbs and Rhymes (Enlarged Edition)	Gordon Wright Publishing	(1986)
Robert Louis Stevenson	Jarrold Colour Publications	(1989)

Greyfriars Bobby
The Real Story at Last

by

Forbes Macgregor

Steve Savage
LONDON AND EDINBURGH

Steve Savage Publishers Ltd
The Old Truman Brewery
91 Brick Lane
LONDON
E1 6QL

www.savagepublishers.com

Published in Great Britain by Steve Savage Publishers Ltd 2002
Reprinted 2003

First published by Gordon Wright Publishing Ltd 1990
Copyright © Forbes Macgregor 1990

ISBN 1-904246-00-1

British Library Cataloguing in Publication Data
A catalogue entry for this book is available from the British Library

Cover illustration: John Haxby

Typeset by Gordon Wright Publishing Ltd, Edinburgh
Printed and bound by The Cromwell Press Ltd

Contents

Portrait of Bobby from life by R W Macbeth in 1868. An etching was made from this portrait by Alexander Wilson in 1918 and copies printed.

Introduction

It may surprise many readers to know that the accepted story of Greyfriars Bobby, as shown on films and television based on Eleanor Atkinson's novel (1912) has been suspect for over a century. Indeed, before Bobby died in 1872 *The Scotsman* stated, regarding a proposed memorial to him, that it hoped the plaque would bear a 'veracious account without fictitious embellishments'.

But that hope was not realised and the inscription on the monument states to this day that 'he lingered near the spot' from 1858 to 1872. The truth is that he roamed all over the district especially as far as Edinburgh Castle though he returned regularly to the grave.

The main part of the story is roughly true but the origins of Bobby and his master are a total myth.

By persevering research in the City archives and other sources of documentary truth, for a year in 1979-80, Forbes Macgregor established beyond any doubt the authentic details of John Gray's life and death as a police constable in the Old Town of Edinburgh.

For many years the Edinburgh Police had known from its records that John Gray was a constable from 1853-58. In 1989, through the help of the Edinburgh Police records, more personal details of John Gray have been published for the first time in one hundred and twenty years. Further recent research by Mr Macgregor in the Greyfriars burial records and other sources has helped to complete the picture.

The framework of the story presented here is fully documented but details from contemporary newspapers of the eighteen fifties and sixties, and from other historical sources have also been used to provide an intriguing and colourful background of life in the Old Town of Edinburgh in the early Victorian era.

G. W.

The Author Wishes to Thank

Edinburgh City Museums for permission to reproduce the photographs on pages 6, 39, 48, 51, 59.

Scottish National Portrait Gallery for permission to reproduce the photograph on page 25.

Miss Elizabeth McConnell of Livingston for permission to reproduce her print of the sketch on page 30.

Edinburgh City Archives for locating the print on page 15.

Mr Peter Blane of Ayr for information on the *Inverness Courier* report.

Mr Iain MacKinnon for information on police matters.

Mr Arnot Beveridge for research into the Valuation Rolls.

Constable Alan L Jeffreys for details of John Gray's enlistment in 1853.

Gordon Wright who took the photographs on pages 17, 37, 42, 52, 55, 57, 59, 63.

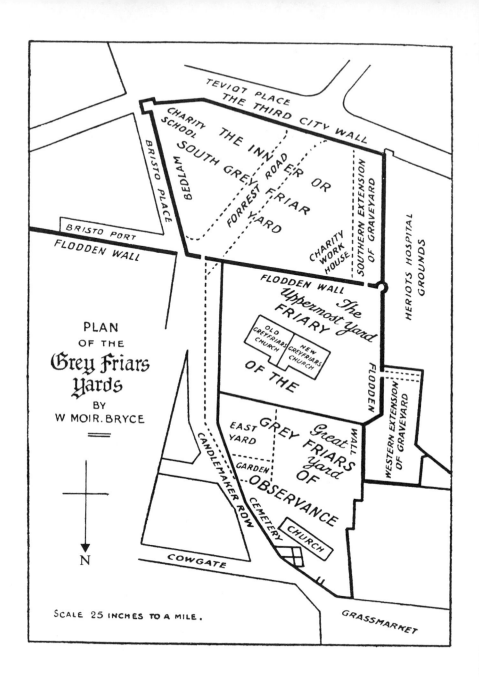

PLAN
OF THE
Grey Friars
Yards
BY
W MOIR. BRYCE

N

SCALE 25 INCHES TO A MILE.

TEVIOT PLACE
THE THIRD CITY WALL

BRISTO PLACE

CHARITY SCHOOL

BEDLAM

THE INN OR

SOUTH GREY

FORREST FRIAR ROAD

YARD

SOUTHERN EXTENSION OF GRAVEYARD

CHARITY WORK HOUSE

HERIOTS HOSPITAL GROUNDS

BRISTO PORT
FLODDEN WALL

FLODDEN WALL

The Uppermost Yard
FRIARY

OLD GREYFRIARS CHURCH

NEW GREYFRIARS CHURCH

OF THE

FLODDEN WALL

WESTERN EXTENSION OF GRAVEYARD

EAST YARD

GREY FRIARS

Great FRIARS Yard

GARDEN

OF

CANDLEMAKER ROW

CEMETERY

OBSERVANCE

CHURCH

COWGATE

GRASSMARKET

8

John Gray Joins the Edinburgh Police

It was Market Day, the last Wednesday of January 1853. A strong south-west wind with squalls of rain and sleet, swept across Edinburgh from the distant Pentland Hills. Between the showers the sun broke through the clouds and people ventured from the shelter of the closes and wynds to purchase goods from the stalls and barrows that lined the great rectangle of the Grassmarket.

Overhung to the north by the high cliffs and grassy slopes of Edinburgh Castle this ancient market place, granted to Edinburgh four centuries before by King James III, occupied a flat valley as large as two football pitches laid end to end. It was enclosed by tall tenements of dwelling-houses, built above rows of shops, taverns and carriers quarters.

The Grassmarket had been the scene of terrible events in the previous two centuries. In the middle of a September night in 1736, a large mob with torches carried the struggling Captain Porteous of the City Guard from the Tolbooth Prison and after hanging him from a dyer's pole, quietly dispersed. Porteous had been granted a pardon by Queen Caroline after causing the death of many innocent people by ordering his men to fire at a mob who had objected to the execution of a popular smuggler.

Much greater injustices and tragedies had been witnessed at the east end of the Grassmarket in the reign of Charles II during the 'Killing Times', when over a hundred innocent martyred Covenanters had been executed on the gallows simply because they wished to worship God in their own way.

All these terrible events had been almost forgotten, although a shocking series of murders only a generation before, had horrified not only Edinburgh but all Britain, when possibly as many as thirty, poor, homeless people were suffocated in Potter's Close, near the Grassmarket, by two Irish thugs called Burke and Hare who sold the bodies to a Dr Knox, for dissection in the medical college.

However, it was now the sixteenth year of the reign of young Queen Victoria, who charmed the folk of Edinburgh by visiting the city every summer and staying in Holyrood Palace with Prince Albert and their large, young family of princes and princesses. A wonderful new age seemed about to dawn. The Great London Exhibition of 1851 had astonished the world by its display of British engineering and manufactures. The 'Hungry 'Forties' had gone, along with its bread cuts and the terrible Irish potato famine. Even memory of the long Napoleonic Wars that had ended in the bloodbath of Waterloo faded after the death in the previous September of the old Duke of Wellington aged eighty-three.

Unfortunately Mother Nature decided to vent her wrath that year and nobody could remember such a winter as the recent months of November, December and January. Gales and rain had lashed the coast of the British Isles. Between three and four hundred shipwrecks had occurred and over two hundred and fifty lives had been lost. The coastguards had been busy night and day, but on the remote coasts of the Atlantic it was impossible to save many poor wretches from the maniac fury of the breakers.

On land, while few lives were lost, all farming and garden work was at a standstill. Potatoes, corn, turnips and other crops could not be harvested; nor could any ploughing or digging be done. Flocks and herds ran short of fodder. Floods added to the misery and the storms blew roofs off houses and barns. The Charity Workhouses or Poorshouses were full of destitute people and thousands of agricultural labourers and their families were penniless and starving.

Amongst the many unemployed who wandered about hoping to find a job of any sort, was John Gray. With his wife and thirteen-year-old son he had come to Edinburgh looking for work as a gardener. His father, also John Gray, had been a gardener and of course had instructed his son in all the tricks of the trade. There were hundreds of country estates in the Borders, in Lothian, Fife and the West country, owned by gentlemen who prided themselves in their walled gardens, in most cases inherited from their ancestors. Scottish gardeners were highly esteemed and many were in charge of large gardens in England including the Royal Gardens of Kew.

Gardening in a large estate employed many labourers as well as the skilled men who looked after the hot-houses where grapes, pineapples, peaches, melons and table flowers were grown at all seasons of the year. 'Auld Jock', as John Gray's father had been known until his death a few years before, was always sought by the large estates as a dependable and skilled workman.

His son, now nicknamed 'Auld Jock' in his turn, was unemployed through no fault of his own. He was desperate for work with a wife and a son to provide for and little left of his last wages.

Outside the magnificent Corn Exchange in the central south side of the Grassmarket, groups of men hoping to be employed as gardeners or labourers had gathered at the feeing place on that Wednesday, early in the morning. But their hopes were dashed. No factors or head gardeners had appeared, for the obvious reason; the ground was unworkable and they were not going to engage men to keep them in idleness.

John Gray, his wife and son, 'Young Jock' had obtained temporary lodgings in a wretched room kept by a cross old crone in a wynd off the West Port, a street leading from the west of the Grassmarket to the large triangle of ground called the Cattle Market, between Lauriston Place and Lady Lawson's Wynd. Here is an eye-witness description of an Edinburgh wynd of the kind where the Grays were finding temporary shelter.

'These wynds were the most wretched features of all. Nobody can

Ballantyne's Close, Grassmarket, 1850.

describe the misery that too obviously dwells there. There is a kind of dirt and wretchedness that foolish people call 'picturesque'. But the greater number of wynds are purgatory to dwell in and not always safe to pass through. Nature does all she can to cleanse the filthy pavement and purify the mouldering walls; blasts of wind whistle through them and deluges of rain pour down them; but not all the rivers of Damascus nor the breezes of

Arabia could sweeten these wretched ravines. As the visitor stoops under the dark cave-like entrance and plunges into the murky twilight of the wynd that he has entered he is disgusted by an atmosphere of poverty which brings fever and pestilence and every ill, moral and physical to which flesh is heir. The blackened, broken windows, stuffed up with clouts of rags, look directly on a blank wall or down on the opposite dweller's misery. Neighbours can shake hands out of the second story or break heads as they are more likely to do, out of the third; for the houses lean over until they almost meet and you look up towards the roofs as through a dark sooty chimney.'

No wonder John Gray was desperate. He had just enough money to purchase a pound or two of potatoes and a few herring from a fishwife, leaving a small sum to pay the rent of the squalid apartment which had neither table nor chair and only a heap of rags to form a bed. A fireplace and an iron pot were the only domestic appliances and some coal remained to provide a litle heat to fend off the January chill.

When he returned with the 'tatties and herring' his wife and son were squatted at the fire. The cooking was primitive. As in thousands of single-ends (one-roomed houses), many of them underground and without windows, the meal was prepared by placing the herring upon the boiling potatoes. The pot was then placed in the middle of the room and the diners sat around and helped themselves with their fingers. There were no plates, knives, forks or even salt or pepper.

'What are we to do?' was the unspoken question as the small family with little appetite ate their dinner. There seemed to be only one answer and nobody had the courage to put it into words, 'The Poorshouse'. It stood to the west of Bristo and immediately behind Greyfriars Kirk and Kirkyard. It was a tall factory-like building of four storeys, with accommodation for about one thousand unfortunates of all ages, from the able-bodied, who were made to work, according to their ability and skill, to those enfeebled by age or disease who sat or lay in apathy or stupor awaiting their release from misery. There was also a hospital or hostel for two hundred children. They were most to be pitied, having no home life and little love bestowed upon them. Some of them were crippled or suffering from other handicaps.

No self-respecting person would think of applying for entry. The Poorshouse was a word of horror and degradation, made even more dismal by being close to a bedlam or madhouse, especially convenient for the benefit of those inmates of the workhouse whom sheer despair or 'natural decay' drove into dementia. It was in this asylum where the unfortunate poet, Robert Fergusson, died in 1774 at the age of twenty-four, tossing in the straw, crying for his mother. Only sheer necessity drove hundreds to the workhouses, of which Edinburgh had three, to wear the degrading workhouse uniform.

In John Gray's time the Greyfriars Charity Workhouse was only half-

The Charity Workhouse, 1820.

full, where five hundred poor souls shared a dole of porridge, bread and soup to keep body and soul together. But some hard-hearted people grudged them even this and wished to send the able-bodied paupers out to delve in the fields or to sweep the street crossings clear of mud, slush or horse-dung in all weathers. This idea was finally rejected by the Governors but the women had to sew and knit, the men had to break firewood or prick oakum or old ropes or work in the kitchen garden. They were allowed two pence out of every shilling they earned, to buy snuff, tobacco or sweets, but were forbidden to buy whisky.

'I wad raither die in a ditch than gang up there,' Auld Jock declared. 'The morn's morning I'll gang an get mysel a job. I've just been thinking o some employ that'll bring us a roof ower oor heids, a steady wage, a suit o claes and respect frae oor freens and neighbours.'

'Then why did ye no think o that afore?' asked Mrs. Gray.

'I hae my ain reasons, woman. Ask nae mair,' he replied, 'I'll let ye ken aboot it the morn.'

And with that, they huddled into the heap of rags that was their bed and tried to pass the long, cold January night as best they could.

At first light about seven o'clock, Auld Jock, without breakfast, gave his face a quick wash in cold water, combed his sandy hair, and set off down the street. He walked smartly up the Grassmarket where at that hour only a few bucket-rakers or 'cinder mavises' were astir, seeking rags, bones or old iron. He climbed the steep slope of the West Bow and made for the High Kirk of

13

St. Giles. To the east of the kirk was the huge block of the Central Police Office. He entered rather hesitantly and was asked his business by the doorkeeper.

'I was thinking o joining the polis,' he muttered.

'Ye'd better come an hae a word wi the inspector,' the man replied.

The inspector looked John up and down and seemed to be pleased with his sturdy appearance.

'Ye seem tae be a man that would stand up tae hard knocks, John. How old are ye?' the inspector asked.

'Forty,' said John.

'We would rather enlist men half yer age,' said the inspector. 'It's no an easy life. But if the surgeon is satisfied wi ye, yer age will no be against ye. We enlisted a man o forty-one a few days ago and he seems tae be shaping up fine. But he was taller than you and desperate tae join as he was married and oot o a job.'

'I'm the same, sir,' said John. 'I hope ye'll be as guid as tae tak me.'

'Away across an see Dr Glover, the surgeon, and let him hae a look at ye,' said the inspector, ending the interview.

Dr Glover ordered John to strip, took his weight and height, sounded him, and nodded. 'You'll do, Mr Gray,' he said. 'Put your clothes on and I'll send the tailor to measure you.'

There was no turning back now. John Gray signed his agreement to the conditions of service without paying much attention to the details. He was told to report the following day to commence his duties as Constable No. 90, warrant No. 1487. His weekly wage, paid in advance, was thirteen shillings, rising to fifteen if he proved his worth.

In the recruitment form which he had signed, the clerk gave a full description of each recruit, none of whom were enlisted unless they had an education and could read, write and count. John Gray's description was: Aged forty, five feet seven and a half inches in height, eleven stone in weight, oval face, grey eyes, sandy hair, fresh complexion, no occupation, married, Scottish. Nobody under five foot seven or much over forty years of age was enlisted. Most of the recruits were Scottish, unmarried and had been labourers, but several were Irish.

Jock was to be provided with a house in the area of his beat in the Tron Parish. It was in the midst of the most densely crowded part of the Old Town in a cul-de-sac called Hall's Court off the Cowgate opposite the High School Wynd. The rent was one shilling per week, deducted from his pay. He also had to pay the same amount towards a Police Outlay Fund which supported local charities.

When Jock returned to the hovel off the West Port at midday, his wife and son did not know whether to laugh or cry.

'Oh Jock, the Coogate!' his wife cried, 'It's fu o naething but thieves an worse. We'll get nae peace there nicht an day. And abody kens hoo thae

An Edinburgh Police Constable in night duty uniform c.1850.

Irishers cairry on when they get a drink in them. They'll fecht wi their shadows. Hall's Court! Ye ken whit a bye-name it's gotten for itsel? 'Hell's Kitchen!'

'Dinna fash yersel, woman!' said Jock, attempting to pacify his wife. 'I hae the hale wecht o the law ahint me noo. I'd like tae see either Scotch or Irish that'll face up tae me. And, forbye, in case ye've forgotten, I'm tae hae a watch-dug that ken's whaur tae meet his teeth.'

'A watch-dug?' said young Jock, suddenly taking an interest.

'Aye,' said his father, 'I'm no shair whit kind, but I suppose it'll hae tae be whit they ca a rough dug. A terrier or a collie maist likely.'

One of the police rules of the day was that each constable had to reside in the area of his beat in case of an emergency such as an accident, a riot or a serious assault. John Gray's beat was the Upper Cowgate, the Grassmarket, Greyfriars Kirkyard, Candlemaker Row, the grounds of Heriot's Hospital and the Cattle Market. It was one of the busiest parts of the Old Town of Edinburgh where there was the greatest temptation for criminals to steal, and where the population was most liable to be drunk and disorderly.

Constables usually patrolled in pairs, each with a watch-dog, but when the sheep and cattle were being gathered into pens on the Sunday, Monday and Tuesday nights before the early morning market on Wednesday, four constables with dogs kept a constant patrol round the market area. They were not allowed a watch-hut nor a brazier fire as this encouraged weaker souls to fall asleep on duty. The night beat was from 10pm. to 6am. Each constable on this long, weary watch was provided with an extra heavy, dark blue greatcoat and a waterproof cape and helmet. He wore a leather belt, and carried a lantern, a baton, a whistle, a rattle to attract attention, a notebook and a pencil. He provided himself with a 'piece' (sandwich) and a flask of tea, coffee or soup to refresh him halfway through his watch. He was forbidden on penalty of instant dismissal and loss of wages, to enter any restaurant or public house. The keeper of the house would also be fined the hefty sum of £5.

In addition to the physical hazards of the night in this lawless part of Edinburgh, there was another threat, even to the most courageous. An hourly patrol of the Greyfriars kirkyard had to be made and each constable was given keys to the upper and lower burial gates.

The Greyfriars Kirkyard had a bad reputation for being haunted by fearful spectres, such as the persecutor of the Covenanters, 'Bloody Mackenzie' and others of dreadful memory. Nobody in the city would venture within its gates after sunset. Nevertheless, the gates were kept locked because the vulnerable back windows of the shops and houses of Candlemaker Row and Greyfriars Place abutted on the east wall of the kirkyard and the joint kirks themselves had historical pewter plate and other valuables. But if a thief was desperate enough, he was willing to dare even the ghouls and ghosts in order to obtain earthly treasure. This was where watchdogs proved their worth, for although a dog's sense of sight is very much weaker than a human's, its power of hearing and scent are infinitely more acute. Even the most cunning and silent of thieves could not escape from the constable's watchdog. In earlier days, before the arrest of Burke and Hare and the execution of Burke, the Greyfriars, like most other kirkyards, was subject to the raids of 'resurrection' men or 'body-snatchers'. Although Burke and Hare were never addicted to grave-robbing, preferring to murder their 'subjects', it was the public outcry at their outrageous crimes that put a stop to the theft of corpses from kirkyards. So John Gray and his fellow officers did not have that extra burden to support.

A rather amusing anecdote concerning the hourly circuit of the Greyfriars both by day and by night, is worth telling if only to show the severity of the police discipline at that time.

Many of the constables were from the Highlands, like the Mackay

16

brothers, Donald, Colin, John and Hugh, all in their twenties, who enrolled at the same time as John Gray. They were natives of Easter Ross and well versed in Gaelic superstitions. It may or may not have been one of them who happened to be on the Greyfriars beat following a light fall of snow.

As he walked slowly down Candlemaker Row just after the witching hour of midnight, he met a police sergeant and lieutenant between the upper and lower gates of the kirkyard.

'Well, constable,' said the sergeant, 'have ye made yer midnight round o the kirkyaird?'

'Aye, indeed, sir,' he replied.

'Well, we'll just tak a stroll among the gravestones and see for oorsels,' said the lieutenant.

The party unlocked the top gate and walked a few paces down the middle path. There was no sign of footprints in the snow.

'Mackay,' said the sergeant, 'for a twelve-stone man, ye've an awfy light step! Call at the head office in the morning.'

Next day he was dismissed without pay.

The following night a less superstitious Highland constable was treated in the same suspicious way but there was no mistaking his footprints in the snow.

'Are ye no afraid o ghosts, Macdonald?' asked the lieutenant.

'No me, sir,' he replied, 'I'm no afraid o anything except lies.' He was not asked to call at the office.

Greyfriars Kirkyard. The two table-stones and John Gray's grave on the left.

A Policeman's Lot is Not a Happy One

John Gray, his wife and son, accompanied by a police sergeant, walked down the crowded, narrow Cowgate towards Hall's Court. Washings fluttered from the clothes-pulleys outside the windows overhead and the pavements were obstructed by all sorts of loiterers; criminals avoiding the police; tattered, dirty, barefoot children, and loud-mouthed women in striped petticoats and tartan shawls, their hair pulled back and fastened with a comb.

They entered Hall's Court by a low archway which had once led to the High Street; but it was now a blind alley. It got its name from a stableman named Hall who kept his horses there.

All the buildings were very old and had been built in a variety of styles, flung together by chance. They seemed to be falling apart but luckily they were only two of three storeys high, unlike the tall tenements in the High Street; great precipices of ten or twelve storeys.

The ground level was occupied by stables for various draught horses, hired out by Hall to draw carts or assist the tram-horses on the steep streets of the city. Their stables were a breeding place for flies, especially in summer, and they were infested by rats and mice that fed on the oats dropped from the horses' troughs. Quite a number of cats lay around the walls, killing time until nightfall when their hunting began.

The tenants of the score of single-room houses hung out of their windows or peeped from behind their curtains to watch the newcomers arrive, for news travelled fast in the Cowgate.

The police house was at the top of a dark, rickety flight of wooden steps. The previous tenants had been turned out because the constable had been dismissed for negligence. They had left the room and bed-recess very dirty. The walls, being in a sub-divided house, were not solid but simply thin, wooden laths papered over. Like all the other Old Town houses, there was no running water and no lavatory. Water had to be carried in pails from a public well at the foot of Blackfriars Wynd or you could employ a caddie to bring a pail of water to your house for a halfpenny. These youths formed an association and performed all sorts of public services. They had a very exact knowledge of the town and kept everyone up to date with the latest news and gossip.

All domestic rubbish was simply thrown out of the windows to be gathered into a heap. When it became so smelly that it could not be endured, it was carted off by the manure workers who were employed by the police, and sold to the farmers to spread on their fields outside the city.

The Grays' first job was to scrub out the house, mend the broken window-

Old houses in the Cowgate near the South Bridge, 1850.

panes and buy in some furniture, including pots and pans, bedclothes, crockery, and cutlery. These were too expensive to buy new, but they could be bought cheaply second or third hand from a well known junk stall in the open air higher up the Cowgate under the shelter of the South Bridge. As it was mainly patronised by Irish it was known as Patrick's or 'Paddy's Market'.

The Grays now had a roof over their heads and John had steady employment. Young Jock also found work as a message-boy. Like most of the children in the Old Town, he did not attend school, which was not compulsory at that time, so he was anxious to earn a few shillings to help his parents.

We have no record of the kind of watchdog Auld Jock was given when he was first recruited. It was probably a rough-haired collie which he kept at home, for they were very popular as working dogs, being highly intelligent, easily trained, affectionate and hardy. Gray was very fond of animals, dogs in particular, and he was accustomed to looking after them. He was often angry when he saw animals ill-treated, for it was part of his duty to accompany either the Inspector of Markets or the Inspector of Nuisances when complaints were received.

A few days after John's enlistment, the weather deteriorated. On 9th February a severe frost set in and heavy snow began to fall and it continued with scarcely a break until the beginning of March. All over Britain it was the worst snowfall since 1838, the first year of Victoria's reign. A train was derailed at Heriot, halfway to Galashiels, by running into a huge drift; all the lochs near Edinburgh were frozen and the streets were barely passable; the Royal Humane Society with ropes, ladders, blankets and hot food and drink attended the frozen lochs in Holyrood Park to rescue skaters and curlers who had 'suffered immersion' and the police were also called in to help.

Around New Year, the whole country had been delighted to read in the newspapers about a marvellous case of what was referred to as 'Canine Fidelity'. The story first appeared in the *Stirling Journal* and was copied by all the other papers, including the *Edinburgh Evening Courant*.

In the Perthshire Highlands, several miles above Loch Katrine, there is a lonely glen called Glen Gyle. It was in the house here that Rob Roy Macgregor was born in 1671. The owner of the house had a number of Dandie Dinmont terriers, these famous little animals that were first bred in the Borders and owing to their colour and their character were named either Mustard or Pepper. A lady visitor to Glen Gyle House took a fancy to one of the Dandie Dinmonts and had him brought by pony and trap to Stirling then by train to Portobello where she lived. The terrier naturally seemed very anxious to escape from his new home, despite every kindness shown to him. A few days after his arrival he escaped by squeezing through a partly opened window. The lady was broken-hearted to find him gone and offered a good reward for his return. Amazingly, a few days after his disappearance from Portobello he turned up, hungry, bedraggled and exhausted at Glen Gyle House. It seemed incredible that he could have found his way on foot over seventy miles of country to a remote Highland glen but the story was well authenticated and believed by people who knew the amazing sense of direction possessed by many animals.

Perhaps John Gray read the story and wished he could have such a faithful canine friend. Little did he know then, that he would soon have a terrier to accompany him on his beat, far more faithful than the Dandie Dinmont.

Each beat lasted eight hours. The morning one was from 6 am. until 2 pm.; the afternoon from 2 pm. to 10 pm. and the night vigil from 10 pm. to 6 am. John was also issued with two greatcoats, a heavy dark blue for night work and a lighter blue for day work. Duties were so arranged that constables enjoyed one free day per week and were not regularly on duty at the same hours. Night duty on the Cattle Market for three nights was followed by afternoon duty for three days.

In the Middle Ages noblemen, merchants, bishops and scholars had inhabited these houses in the Old Town but, after the splendid New Towns of North and South Edinburgh had been built at the end of the eighteenth century, the Old Town of the High Street, Canongate and Cowgate with its many closes, wynds and courts had been sub-divided and let to the thousands of poor folk who crowded the streets. their numbers were swelled by many Highland and Irish country people who left their turf cabins and black houses to find work in the Lowlands of Scotland and finished off worse than they had started. They crowded into single rooms, often as many as twenty together, with no privacy, beds or sanitation, living worse than cattle. The only relief from their misery was a plentiful supply of cheap, illicit whisky or Irish 'poteen', the latter a raw spirit fermented from potatoes or oats.

On Saturdays and Sundays, great numbers regularly got drunk and the Cowgate became a battlefield as men and women cursed and brawled until they collapsed insensible. The police then sprang into action. A long windowless wagon sarcastically named 'The Black Maria' arrived, drawn by two horses. The constables lifted the unconscious bodies into the wagon and carted them up the Cowgate to a prison specially built about 1830 for the convenience of that inebriated district.

They were put in cells and charged when sober with being drunk and incapable. Those who decided to fight the police, and many did, soon regretted it for they were man-handled into a Black Maria and later charged with being drunk and disorderly. There were thousands of men and as many women arrested in the Old Town each year and many wretched creatures appeared in court over a hundred times. Constable Gray sometimes had to help lift as many as twenty drunks from the pavement on a Saturday night.

Only by living in the midst of such squalor did John Gray realise what an impossible job he had taken on.

Drunkenness was easy to deal with, but that was the least of police worries for they had a good deal of assistance from the local priests who severely reprimanded members of their flock who yielded to the temptation of drink. But even the threat of hellfire did not stop most of them from forgetting their misery for a few hours for as little as a shilling or less. One old Irishwoman, rebuked by the father, excused herself by saying, 'Sure I never intinded to fall from grace but it being so mortal chill, the smell of the drink from the pub came over me weary soul like the waft of an angel's wing'.

If poverty and starvation drove people to commit crime, the severe punishment they risked if discovered did not deter them. In Edinburgh the most common sentence was a long term of imprisonment in the Calton Jail, a very imposing building with romantic ornamental towers on the top of a cliff on the Calton Hill, which visitors often mistook for Edinburgh Castle. But it was far from splendid inside where the prisoners were put in narrow cells, six feet by eight, fed on a ration of bread and porridge and only allowed a short period of exercise in the courtyard each day. 'The female prisoners,' as Stevenson says, 'taking their exercise like a string of nuns'. If they misbehaved they were put on the treadmill where they were forced to trudge upon a moving wheel without a halt until all the mischief was worn out of them.

In the first week or two of John Gray's service there were reports in the *Edinburgh Evening Courant* describing the sort of crimes that were punished by a long spell in jail. A man stole a packet of boot-tackets from a shoemaker in the High Street and was sentenced to sixty days hard labour.

Transportation was reserved for 'less trivial' offences. Sentenced to a term of seven years, or a double term of fourteen years, the prisoner was taken to a seaport, usually on the Thames or the Mersey and put aboard a sailing ship which was actually a floating prison. Crowded below decks without sanitation or proper food and drink, these unfortunates spent up to three months on a dangerous voyage to Australia or Tasmania from which they were unlikely to return.

In the High Court of Justiciary at Edinburgh on the 1st February 1853, the very day John Gray was recruited, a miserable woman named Ann Goodwin who had stolen two bedgowns and a child's frock from a clothes-line was sentenced to seven years transportation. In the same court that day, in the name of justice, a violent woman named Elizabeth Wilson who had stabbed a neighbour, Catherine Stewart, in the neck and chest to the danger of her life, was given the same sentence as the petty thief who perhaps needed the clothing for her poor family.

The police had also to deal with accidents. On 14th February, St Valentine's Day, poor Mary Whiteside, who lived several storeys up in a close in the Canongate, fell down the stairs and broke her neck. A week later on 22nd February, not far away in White Horse Close, Susan MacLeod was burnt to death.

In the second year of Auld Jock's service, in the same area, a great section of an ancient wall fell down, destroying a nearby house and crushing four little children. Two died and two were maimed for life. Such events were not unusual in a town crumbling to decay.

College Wynd, opposite Hall's Court in the Cowgate.

The police must have wished a similar accident on some of the 'lands' or tenements where the occupants spent their lives either plotting crimes or putting them into effect.

Robert Louis Stevenson says 'One night I went along the Cowgate after everyone was abed but the policeman, and stopped by hazard before a tall 'land'. The moon touched upon its chimneys and shone blankly upon the upper windows; there was no light anywhere in the great bulk of building; but as I stood there it seemed to me that I could hear quite a body of quiet sounds from the interior; doubtless there were many clocks ticking, and people snoring on their backs . . . the whole pile beating in time to its time-pieces like a great disordered heart.'

Another similar tenement seemed to him to be 'breathing out evil'. 'The Happy Land' at the head of the Canongate was such a place. It was the haunt of the worst criminals.

Taking everything into account, the police were kept busy and John Gray must have earned his thirteen shillings several times over, each week.

Over these scenes of human degradation there usually hung a thick pall of coal smoke which earned Edinburgh the title 'Auld Reekie' as it was visible as far away as the shores of Fife. Every evening as the great blue cloud arose from the Old Town like the dust-cloud from a volcano, the country folk timed their suppers from its regular appearance. It may have been amusing and romantic from a distance but it was unpleasant and unhealthy to live amongst. The Lothian coalfield was only a mile or two distant so coal was

23

cheap and cost only sixpence to tenpence per hundredweight. Small shops in the Canongate sold it at a halfpenny per pail. The chimneys soon became choked with soot and as a sweep charged fourpence to clean the chimney few people sent for him. Fourpence bought a pound of meat, a dozen eggs, a pound of sugar or two pounds of candles. In 1856 a four pound loaf cost sixpence-halfpenny.

The best way to clean the 'lum' was to put a flaming newspaper up to burn the soot, with the result that a great, yellow, acrid cloud of smoke descended over the entire neighbourhood making everyone cough and splutter.

Tuberculosis and typhus were the main killers, carrying off a victim on average every six hours. The death rate amongst the hundred thousand inhabitants in the square mile of this vast rabbit warren was forty-five per thousand per year giving a life expectancy of a little over twenty years. In the centre of Edinburgh, in the High Kirk district, only one person in each hundred and twenty reached the alloted span of three score and ten.

Edinburgh could be unbearably hot in July and bitterly cold at any time between November and March. The easterly 'haar' or sea-fog often spoilt the early summer for days at a time. This dense, chilly, soaking mist reduced visibility to a few yards and was made more noxious as it was always accompanied by an intolerable stink picked up as it passed from the Firth of Forth over the extensive irrigation meadows of Craigentinny which were fertilised continuously by being submerged in the raw sewage of the city. They produced five crops of grass each year to feed the thousands of dairy cows, mostly consumptive, kept in byres all over the town.

Police conditions of service were rigorously enforced. Instant dismissal was the result of negligence or misconduct. It was little wonder that very few officers lasted more than two years. A number left after a year, being dismissed, or after giving a month's notice, resigning. Exceptionally determined men, refusing to be enticed by the £4. bounty offered by the Army (anxious to recruit for the imminent war with Russia in the Crimea), served for as long as four years. When John Gray died on 8th February 1858 after, almost to the day, a service of five years, he was the longest serving constable of all the thirty men who enlisted from September 1852 to April 1853, except Robert MacPherson, who also served five years and significantly, also died prematurely aged only thirty-one. In other words, any constable conscientious enough to endure the harsh conditions for five years ran a grave risk of dying from exposure, not entirely to the elements, but to conditions of service. Most of those who left the police service, either voluntarily or by order, probably joined the army or navy where conditions were much more attractive.

An interesting incident, which has a direct bearing upon John Gray, concerns the short service of P.C. 273, Alexander Farquhar, who was recruited on 27th July 1855 at the age of twenty-five. At one stage he was allowed the large sum of £2. to replace his watch-dog which perhaps through negligence on his part he had lost. At any rate he was not rated very highly as a policeman and dismissed after sixteen months. Besides proving that officers were obliged to have a watch-dog, this incident also gives us leave to speculate whether losing a watch-dog counted as negligence or misconduct.

John Gray acquired his world-famous Skye terrier sometime about 1856, or so it would seem if we argue backwards from Bobby's death on 14th January 1872 to that year, and assume that Bobby had attained old age at sixteen years. He was probably about six months old when Gray took him into his care and at that age required a licence as the authorities did not regard him as a puppy any more. How Gray lost his first dog, whether by rabies or distemper, by illness brought on by long exposure or by theft or accident, shall never be known. What is certain is that he had been obliged to have a watch-dog from February 1853 until he acquired a substitute about two years before his own death in February 1858.

But here we must open a new chapter as the most important actor, however short in the leg, enters the stage.

Bobby, by an unknown photographer.

Enter Bobby, the Skye Terrier Puppy

The first problem for the Grays was what to call their new puppy. Several names were suggested. Robert Burns' 'Twa Dogs' were Luath and Caesar, Walter Scott's dog was Maida. None of these seemed to fit. What about Toby in the Punch and Judy shows? That was also rejected. At last Young Jock cried out, 'It's staring us in the face. He's a polis watch-dog. We'll ca him 'Bobby' for that's what a' the bairns cry efter faither. 'Here comes Bobby, keekin' in the lobby.' And so it was agreed, without further argument.

The new Police force had been started by Sir Robert Peel, the Prime Minister, about twenty years before and at first it was very unpopular. Officers were insulted in the street. Their tall hats and frock coats were ridiculed. They were made fun of in all sorts of ways and nicknamed 'Peelers' or 'Bobbies' after their founder. But as crime decreased, they soon began to win respect. So in 1856, Bobby was not such a bad name to be called and soon the wee Skye terrier learned to answer to it.

Bobby now became the greatest source of pleasure in John Gray's life. His legs were barely six inches long and his shaggy hair hung over his eyes and from his long body. He had only a stump of a tail and it wagged continually as he chased up and down, prepared to start a fight with any dog large or small. He would even square up to a mastiff which, luckily for Bobby, merely looked contemptuously down its nose at him. Many of these very large dogs, wolfhounds, great Danes, St Bernards as well as bloodhounds, were masked or muzzled, especially when there was fear of rabies in the town, a dreadful disease also known as hydrophobia. Some ignorant people seemed to sense danger in every dog, large or small and were only too eager to shout 'Mad dog!' sending people scurrying for their lives.

But Skye terriers differ from most other dogs in at least three ways. A famous nature writer and sportsman named Charles St John, who wrote about his Skye terriers a few years before Bobby's birth, said that they had a most peculiar habit of running on three legs with one hind leg up in the air as if keeping it in reserve for an emergency. They would also lie quietly for hours under a bank or bush without moving or showing the least sign of impatience. Their third peculiarity, which of course was very convenient for John Gray's slender purse, was that they had no fads about what they ate. They liked bread, rolls, porridge, buns or sweets, but dog-like, a juicy piece of steak, raw or cooked, was a real treat.

The entire race of terriers, which consists of dozens of different breeds, are known for their strong, keen sense of smell which enables them to detect their prey through several feet of soil. Their name is derived through French from the Latin *terra*, the earth. The French is *terriere*. Scotch terriers, Cairns, Highland, Skye or Dandie Dinmonts are all known to the French as *terrieres griffon*. Owing to their ferocity and tenacity they remind us of that mythical creature, the griffon, which has the wings of an eagle and the hindquarters and claws of a lion.

Terriers also love to scrape a hollow in the earth and prefer to lie there rather than in a kennel or basket.

There were three markets which the Edinburgh police had to supervise. The Cattle Market was held early on the Wednesday morning some distance away to the south-west of the Grassmarket in a large triangle of ground filled by pens.

A market mainly for sheep and lambs was held on Mondays eight miles from Edinburgh on the foothills of the Pentland Hills at House o' Muir near the battlefield of Rullion Green. A wagon took six policemen out to this remote spot to see that no disturbance or crime took place, as a lot of money changed hands and attracted thieves, pick-pockets and highway robbers.

The general market for all sorts of provisions and miscellaneous merchandise was held on Wednesday beneath the Castle Rock in the Grassmarket, where thousands of town and country folk thronged the great rectangle from morning to night.

There were soldiers from the Castle and from the various barracks outside the town. Some wore kilts and spoke Gaelic, which the townsfolk

The Grassmarket and Edinburgh Castle in Victorian times.

could not understand; others wore trews or trousers either of tartan or plain cloth. Equally colourful were the fishwives from Newhaven and their rivals from Fisherrow, vying with one another to sell their wares. Both wore several striped petticoats of pink, blue and white, with dark blue skirts. They had strong tuneful voices as they cried 'Caller herrin! Caller haddies! Caller ou!' You can guess the first two, the last meant fresh oysters, dragged that morning from the large oyster bed in the River Forth between Leith and the island of Inchkeith. Oysters are expensive nowadays but at that time they cost only twenty pence a hundred.

Old wives with handcarts, laden with leeks, carrots, turnips, cabbages and onions shouted to would-be customers to buy a bawbees-worth (a halfpenny-worth) of mixed vegetables to make broth. In summer there were great baskets of strawberries, pails of cream and bunches of roses. Other hawkers sold candy, toffee apples, bulls-eyes and peppermint lumps. Candles, coal, old clothes, boots, pots and pans, string and rope were all for sale, mixter-maxter. In early spring, American russet and red apples and Spanish Seville oranges were plentiful and cheap. Eggs, butter, cheese and poultry were also in good supply.

John Gray met many friends on market day, both at the general market and the Cattle Market. He was well-liked as a policeman because he made a point of settling quarrels between neighbours and cautioning people who might be tempted to steal or get into debt.

Bobby kept close to his master's heels at the markets. He never quarrelled with bitches, but he was always keen to argue with male dogs. There is an old saying, 'Dogs delight to bark and fight' and Bobby did both. Dog fights were very common on market days, because the town dogs objected to the country dogs taking over their territory and lowered their heads, stiffened their tails and growled at the strangers. Their owners tried to stop them, either by shouting their names sharply, or dealing them a sharp rap with a walking stick or shepherd's crook. But they often had to be pulled apart by the tails or hind legs.

Some men and boys loved a good dog-fight. The shout, 'A dog-fight, come on!' always drew a crowd. But John Gray never encouraged Bobby to make a public exhibition of himself. He had to reserve his energies for his duties.

If Auld Jock and Bobby had been on night duty at the Cattle Market they returned to Hall's Court after 6 am. where Bobby had a bowl of bread and milk while his master changed into civilian clothes. After a rest, they strolled up the Cowgate, or perhaps took a 'dander' or leisurely walk returning to arrive at Greyfriars Place where, about midday, they took a seat in the Coffee House kept in 1856 and 1857 by Mr William Ramsay who lived at the back of the shop.

Bobby and his master were always welcome. They had a favourite seat in the corner and watched Mrs Ramsay as she bustled in and out of the backroom where she baked pies, made soup and infused tea and coffee. Bobby knew he would be given a bun, a dish of stew or a piece of pie, and sometimes he was awarded a meaty bone from the soup pot.

After dinner the pair of them sauntered off down Candlemaker Row towards Cowgatehead, in no hurry to reach Hall's Court with its squalor, smell of horse dung, noisy children, quarrelsome neighbours and the high pitched screech of a neighbouring sawmill.

Night duty at the Cattle Market was not very pleasant. The policemen and watch-dogs had to keep on the move round the pens of sheep, pigs and cattle to prevent theft. The weather was often wet, cold, windy or snowing and they felt a great temptation to seek shelter in the restaurant which stood in the middle of the market. But police were not permitted to relax there. It was crowded with drovers, shepherds and farmers, eating, drinking and laughing or sometimes quarrelling. They were a very rough lot, for they led a coarse life, driving their animals along the drove roads which ran through the hills towards Edinburgh and usually sleeping in the open beside their beasts in all weathers. The inn was also full of sheep dogs who would not have put up with Bobby had he mixed with them.

The area surrounding the market had also to be patrolled in case any suspicious characters were lurking there and it was very eerie to walk through the deserted streets in what were called 'the wee sma oors o the nicht', that is, one, two or three o'clock in the morning. Bobby and Auld Jock were glad when dawn came and they could go home and take a bite of breakfast before the coal fire.

There were occasions of public rejoicing in the town when everybody joined in. One of these took place in the Grassmarket on 31st October 1856, which was Hallowe'en, always a night of great excitement all over Scotland, when toffee, apples and nuts were enjoyed and all kinds of games were played. This particular celebration however, was a national rejoicing to mark the end of the Crimean War. In Edinburgh it was called the 'Great Crimean Banquet' and was held in the Corn Exchange attended by soldiers of various regiments, infantry, artillery and engineers, who had returned after the long war. Huge crowds joined in the rejoicing; bonfires were lit on the hill-tops and in the streets and bands played well into the night.

By the summer of 1857 Bobby had grown accustomed to his duties and was firmly attached to his master, following him to his favourite haunts around the town. A strange thing about Edinburgh was the fact that a ten minutes walk from the most unhealthy part of the Old Town brought one to the fresh air and sunshine of Holyrood Park, Arthur's Seat and Salisbury Crags where sheep grazed on the ancient turf and skylarks and meadow pipits sang from the sky. In early summer, the great banks of whin were golden with nut-scented blossom, while bluebells and wild roses grew among the rocks. There was no need to stay in the dirt and smoke, and many women of the Cowgate and Canongate carried their laundry up to the

From Life

A sketch of Bobby from life.

Calton Hill or down to Holyrood Park where there were wells and fixed clothes poles where they could wash and dry their clothes.

Bobby liked to chase his shadow over the flowery turf and he was excited when he roused a rabbit from its lair on the long grass. But the rabbits were too fast for him and bolted into their burrows among the roots and rocks.

All over Britain, however, people had more to think about than the joys of summer. Every day brought fresh news of murder and unbelievable savagery from India where the Sepoys or native soldiers had mutinied and killed not only their British officers but white women and children.

The 78th Regiment, or Seaforth Highlanders, were stationed in Edinburgh Castle and like many other troops they were ordered to embark for India. At that time they grew great bushy beards, wore bearskin helmets and of course spoke Gaelic. They were nicknamed 'The Wild MacRaas' or MacRaes as most of the regiment were from that clan. In 1778 they had caused a great sensation because, protesting at being sent to America to fight the colonists, they rebelled and marched in a body to the summit of Arthur's Seat where they dug trenches, which may still be seen, to defend themselves. The Edinburgh people supported them and took food, drink and blankets up to the camp which later they abandoned on promises of better treatment which, shameful to say, were soon broken.

One summer morning in 1857 they marched away from Edinburgh Castle to the docks at Leith to the skirl of the bagpipes and boarded troopships for Bombay, anxious to avenge the atrocities committed on some of their own people. After a long sea-voyage they were thrown into the thick of the fighting in the scorching Indian summer. By the autumn, the Edinburgh newspapers reported that, out of eight hundred Highland men who had left Edinburgh, less than half survived.

Auld Jock was saddened to hear this, because some of the regiment had been his friends in the police force.

Meantime, Bobby had learned a few words of the human language, such as 'walkies', 'bone', 'good doggy' and 'Bobby'. He also knew that when his master pointed to a certain place and said, 'Bobby, on trust,' he had to lie there quite still, watching everyone who came near, and barking sharply if anyone tried to handle him.

Of the three hundred and thirty men in the Edinburgh City and County Police, about one third who were not on duty performed their drill in the Grassmarket if the weather was fair; if wet, they drilled in the Corn Exchange undercover. Bobby with all the other watch-dogs lay on the steps of the various buildings, or at the edge of the Corn Exchange hall and watched the constables marching, turning and wheeling about to the sharp commands of the Superintendant. When drill was over, Constable Gray took Bobby for a walk, pleased with his behaviour and patted him, giving him a piece of bread and cheese because he had lain so patiently waiting for him.

Nobody at that time had any idea how soon it would be before wee Bobby put himself on trust to await his master in a quite different, not so pleasant place, only a few hundred yards away.

The Corn Exchange, Grassmarket.

31

Bobby is Puzzled by Strange Happenings

In October 1857, the nights were cold and wet and Auld Jock and Bobby were often soaked and shivering. When they dried off before the glowing coal fire at Hall's Court they sent up clouds of steam. Auld Jock had developed a nasty cough which worried his wife and son, but Bobby grew accustomed to it and it didn't bother him as he lay by the fire in his basket and barked softly and whimpered in his sleep.

Young Jock and his mother watched Bobby and laughed. 'He thinks he's chasing rabbits amang the whins on Arthur's Seat,' said Mrs Gray. Perhaps she was right.

Later in the year, Auld Jock's cough got much worse so he reported to Dr Littlejohn when he felt unable to continue his duties. Dr Henry Littlejohn was Police Surgeon, a young man, small of stature but very energetic. He had succeeded Dr Glover in August 1854 and knew John Gray's good record as a constable. In November the doctor called at Hall's Court. He examined Jock as he lay back in his armchair, and looked serious.

'I'll report that you are unfit for duty until further notice, Jock. I'm sorry to tell you that you won't be allowed full pay of fifteen shillings.'

'That's nae faut o yours, doctor. We'll jist hae to mak ends meet as best we can.'

'I've known you well enough over these last four years to respect you, Jock. I'll do my best to get you back on duty.'

The police messenger brought the Grays' seven shillings each Friday for the next six weeks and although Young Jock was working, every penny of income was spent on food, coal and small luxuries for the invalid.

In a visit before Christmas Dr Littlejohn brought some fresh eggs and fruit. 'See that Jock gets plenty nourishing food,' he said. 'Herrings are better than meat, and cheaper. On fine days he should take Bobby for a walk in the park.'

'What's wrang wi him, doctor?' Mrs Gray asked shakily.

'It's a bad chill brought on by the night air,' said the doctor.

'It's naethin serious, doctor, is it?' she went on.

Dr Littlejohn hesitated, 'Well, we'll hope not. But this dirty smoky town won't help him.'

'Can ye no gie him a bottle?' she pleaded.

'Yes, of course, I'll write a line for the druggist to give you something to ease his cough.'

The doctor scribbled out a prescription and wished them 'Good afternoon,' patting Bobby's head and telling him to be a good dog and guard his master well. He felt saddened by his lack of power to cure John Gray for he was quite aware that he was ill with a prevalent disease for which there was little hope of a cure. We call it tuberculosis, but the doctors in Bobby's time named it by the strange Greek word *phthisis* or the wasting disease. The common people called it a decline or consumption. Countless thousands, young and old, died of it. A peculiarity of this illness, was that many who had it did not feel ill. They were bright and cheerful and full of good humour. Every day they felt they would soon throw it off. Their eyes were bright, their cheeks flushed and their skin clear, but those who knew these signs were not deceived. The only hope of a cure was to go to some warm climate, or to pure mountain air. But how many could afford that? Certainly not poor John Gray.

The family was grateful for the sick allowance and Young Jock's wages prevented them from being forced to apply for assistance to the Charity Workhouse.

All through the merry days of New Year, 1858, known as the 'Daft Days', everyone did their best to enjoy themselves. Edinburgh folk gathered at the Tron Kirk, just a short walk up the hill from Hall's Court and the Cowgate, in the last hours of the dying year, 1857. When they heard the faint chimes of the church clock strike the hour of midnight they cheered and shook hands with friends and strangers alike, capering and dancing as they made their way to first-foot all their neighbours. They sang *Auld Lang Syne* and wished each other a Happy New Year, convinced for the moment that the New Year would be happy and prosperous for everybody, man, woman and child.

John Gray took Dr Littlejohn's advice. He and Bobby walked for an hour or two on fine days. The bottle of cough mixture seemed to ease his irritation. Most days they walked up the Cowgate to the Grassmarket, especially on Market Day and on to Ramsay's eating house. Everyone kindly asked Auld Jock how he was. They said he looked very fit. They expected him back on duty very soon. Jock smiled and said he would be back, no doubt, by the spring.

But on Candlemas Day, 2nd February, he was not able to rise. His wife helped him to the fireside. He sat for a time but said he was so tired he would be better lying down. Bobby lay at his feet and looked up at him with sad watchful eyes. Auld Jock called him to come nearer, stroked his wise little head and murmured 'Poor wee Bobby. You'd like to go walkies, wouldn't you?'

Bobby sat up on his hind legs and barked softly. Then when he saw that his master was asleep, he put his head between his front paws and dozed off.

On Sunday 7th February, Dr Littlejohn called to see his patient.

'Well, Jock, how is the man today? I expected to see you away up to Greyfriars to hear Dr Lee preach. We're having a fine spell of weather.'

Jock smiled weakly. 'Doctor, to tell you the truth, my legs are as weak as water. I've a bad catch in my breath as weel. Ye'll excuse me no gettin up.'

Welcoming the New Year at the Tron Kirk.

'That's all right Jock. You lie and rest. I walked over from York Place on another call. I just wanted a word with you and your good wife, not forgetting wee Bobby.'

'Doctor, I mind the day I joined the force when Dr Glover passed me as a very fit man. What an awfy change thae five years hae made on me. I fear I'll no be on my feet again. And how many will remember me when I'm lying up yonder in the Heich Yaird?'

'Folk are very forgetful, Jock, but this much I am certain of—wee Bobby will never forget your kindness as long as he lives.'

The kind young doctor did not stay long. He wished them 'good morning' and went about his business down into the Cowgate.

The kirk bells of Edinburgh were calling the faithful. The ladies in dark Sabbath crinolines, and the gentlemen, with Sunday black suits and tall hats, were gathering to worship God. It was such a fine bracing day, with the salty wind from the sea and the birds singing, that everyone sang the psalms and hymns loudly and cheerfully.

Next day, John Gray's condition deteriorated. Bobby lay at the foot of his bed. Every few minutes he looked up, expecting his master to get up for dinner then go for a walk.

The sun blinked in, throwing a pale light across the room. Shouts of children at play came from the court, and the high-pitched noises of the sawmill filled the air now and again.

Dinner-time was long past, but Mrs Gray remembered Bobby and gave him a few bites of bread and cheese.

Shortly after five o'clock darkness fell. Mrs Gray lit a candle and put it on the table. Bobby left the bed and lay by the fire, for he knew that there would be no walks that evening.

Young Jock came home from work and in a whisper asked how his father was. Mrs Gray shook her head.

At a quarter to nine, Constable John Gray ended his duties in this world.

In the first morning light Young Jock went down to John Raeburn the undertaker's shop in the Cowgate to ask him to make urgent arrangements for his father's funeral, as there was no room in the house for both the living and the dead.

Throughout the following night Mrs Gray, Young Jock and Bobby sat by the fire, the candles burning low and new ones being lit. It was an old custom to sit up all night in the room where the dead lay and keep candles constantly burning. It was called a 'wake' and the idea was to ward off evil spirits. Now and then Mrs Gray made a cup of tea to keep them from falling asleep. Bobby got a piece of bread and butter. He sensed that something strange and unusual was going on but he did not know what it was. He often looked at the long wooden box and whimpered as if to ask, 'Why have they put my master in that queer bed?'

Wednesday, 10th February, was a busy day. John Raeburn, the undertaker had not been idle. He had visited Greyfriars Kirkyard to see Bailie James Campbell, the Mortality Recorder, who kept a record of all burials. A piece of ground was purchased for John Gray's grave. It had to be in the Heich Yard because Gray was resident in the district of St Giles and

35

had a right to be buried besides Greyfriars Kirk. The Greyfriars gardener, James Brown, had known Auld Jock and he helped to choose a good site for the grave in the shelter of two enormous table-stones beside the main path.

The head graveman was old John Haywood but he was not present as he was lying at home very ill. His assistant, James Dunn, took over his duties although he was well over seventy. Luckily, he had hired two strong young gravemen who were quite pleased to earn a day's wages. In a short time they had dug the grave to the required depth. James Brown did not dig graves but his job was to see that everything was neatly done. In his youth he had had a good training as a gardener at Dalkeith, seven miles from Edinburgh. He knew all about plants and trees and kept the Kirkyard in repair, pruning the ornamental shrubs and lopping large branches off the sycamore and ash trees that grew rapidly in the rich soil of the Greyfriars.

In the previous century the yard had been allowed to grow wild, but there was no untidiness in James Brown's time. The grass was regularly cut by skilled men with scythes and shears. The edges of the paths and graves were trimmed. The gravestones were not allowed to fall over. And, more important, the gates were locked to keep out children and dogs.

The Burial Gate and the steps leading up into the kirkyard were at the foot of Candlemaker Row near some quaint old houses known as the Cunzie Neuk. These gates and steps had been completely renewed in 1854. The other larger gate was at the top of the Row close to Ramsay's Eating House. The Burial Gate was only opened for funerals. The Kirk Gate was opened for Church services.

John Gray's funeral set off from Hall's Court in the forenoon about eleven o'clock. All the neighbours turned out to watch the policemen shoulder the coffin and carry it up the Cowgate. A large number of police constables who were off duty formed a procession behind the coffin, following Young Jock and a few friends. But, almost unnoticed, there was another mourner trotting alongside Young Jock. It was wee Bobby.

When the procession reached the Cowgatehead, the weekly market was in full swing. It was a fine sunny day and everyone was enjoying the spell of settled weather. The fisher-lassies cried their wares, the small boys yelled and the collies and terriers yelped back at them. The Cattle Market had finished hours before and the farmers and drovers had joined the crowd in the Grassmarket.

Bobby's tail began to wag with joy. He was going to the market after all. But his pleasure was short-lived. The funeral turned up Candlemaker Row.

'Oh' thought Bobby, 'we're going up to the pie and bone shop.' His tail began to wag again.

But no, the policemen carrying the coffin stopped at the Burial Gate. The usher, inside, unlocked it and four men carying two batons came out. They put the two strong wooden batons under the coffin to take it from the men who were shouldering it. The usher, who wore a long frock coat and black

36

trousers, had a tall, black, silk hat with a black veil hanging from it over his shoulders. He had a very serious face and carried a black baton like a long police truncheon. He unfolded a beautifully ornamented cloth and covered the entire coffin. This was called the mort-cloth and it was hired out by the church to hide the bare wooden coffin. The charge for the mort-cloth was used to help poor people.

The procession, led by the usher, climbed slowly up the nineteen steep steps to the path that led to where the grave awaited. James Campbell the recorder was there. Dr Robert Lee, the minister of Greyfriars, conducted the burial service because John Gray had been one of his congregation. The prayers ended and with the final words 'Dust to dust, ashes to ashes', the minister dropped a handful of soil into the grave and the gravemen began to shovel in the earth.

Bobby had lain quietly watching this strange scene. What were all these men doing to his beloved master? Why were they putting him into that deep hole? How long would he be down there? Bobby could not understand it at all. It had never happened before.

Everyone turned away and walked back to the gate, leaving the gravemen to their work. Young Jock picked up Bobby and despite his struggles carried him down the Cowgate and back to Hall's Court. Bobby did not want to leave his master but he was gripped very firmly and soon, unwillingly, he found himself back home.

The Burial Gate at Greyfriars.

Bobby's Long Watch Begins

Mrs Gray and a few friendly neighbours stayed at home and prepared a funeral tea while the men folk attended the burial, as women did not attend burials in Scotland at that time.

One of the police regulations of the day was that each member of the force had to contribute sixpence towards the funeral of a policeman; fourpence for the funeral of a policeman's wife and twopence for a policeman's child. So Auld Jock's widow had over £8. to cover the funeral expenses and provide a suitable tea for the mourners. This farewell tea was a custom which was always observed and any family, however poor, was disgraced if they refused to provide food and drink at funerals, baptisms or weddings, although some had to starve themselves for days after, because of the expense.

The small table in the Grays' home was neatly laid with boiled ham, tongue, bread, cheese, cake and jam and there was whisky and tea to wash it down.

But one small mourner had no appetite. Bobby lay growling under the table, refusing to eat anything. Some kind folk tried to pat him, but he edged away and growled worse than ever.

Then he did something that he had never done before. He stretched out his legs, raised his head and howled.

'Oh stop that, Bobby,' cried Mrs Gray. 'Dinna let us hae ony mair o that. Ye're pittin us tae shame.'

But it made no difference. Bobby howled louder than ever.

Now, a dog howling was thought to be a very bad omen. It was a warning of death and the neighbours on all sides separated only by thin partitions, complained by knocking on the walls. Everyone was irritated at Bobby's behaviour so they were relieved when he stopped and lay sulking under the table.

The gathering continued into the evening. Candles were lit and the guests settled down to enjoy an evening of conversation refreshed by cups of tea and glasses of whisky.

Bobby was as patient as he could be but, at last, he got up and began to scratch at the door. He wanted out of this place where nobody seemed to care about him.

At last Young Jock opened the door and Bobby scampered down the crooked stairs, across the Court, into the Cowgate and away up the crowded smelly streets as fast as his legs could carry him.

Bobby knew where he was going and soon arrived at the Greyfriars Burial Gate and tried to squeeze between the iron bars, but they were deliberately made narrow to keep dogs out. He tried to scrape beneath them but there was a stone step. He ran up Candlemaker Row to the main Kirk Gate, which he had often entered when on patrol with Auld Jock. But it was also locked and impossible to get through.

After a few minutes the many church clocks began to strike the hour. Bobby was not a good counter, but it was ten o'clock, when the police made their first night round of the Kirkyard.

To his delight two policemen appeared walking up the short lane to the large gate where they paused and unlocked it. They did not notice Bobby, for it was very dark, so he quickly slipped in and was soon hidden amongst the tombstones.

'Did ye notice something flash past, Dugald?' asked one.

'No unless it was a ghost coming back frae a visit tae the public-hoose,' replied the other with a chuckle.

'This is no a place tae be joking aboot ghosts,' said his friend. 'I wouldna like tae be left here mysel in this city o the deid in a dark, moonless nicht like this.'

The policemen walked round behind the kirks, flashing their lanterns on the doors and windows. Satisfied that no burglars had tried to break in, they left by the Burial Gate, locking it behind them. Bobby was left alone in the graveyard.

Bobby knew at once where his master was buried. When he found the partly-filled grave, he quietly lay down on the boards that covered it.

Portrait of Bobby from life by Gourlay Steell, R.S.A., 1867.

It was a pitch-black night as the moon was not due to rise until an hour before sunrise. A cold sea-wind began to blow after midnight and the stars were blotted out by low clouds. A few chilly showers forced Bobby to seek shelter under the table-stone beside his master's grave. He was quite dry there but very cold as the wind blew strongly under the great stone roof.

It was a stroke of good luck for Bobby that Auld Jock's grave had been dug close to two great table-stones. It was very likely that James Brown had deliberately chosen such a site to enable Young Jock and his mother to easily find the grave because they certainly had not enough money to put up a stone to mark it.

The stones where Bobby sheltered had been there for many years. The higher one was put up in the year of the battle of Waterloo to commemorate a woman called Jean Grant and it is inscribed with a text from the Bible— which may well apply to Bobby. 'With such sacrifices God is well pleased.'

What a long night it was. After a time Bobby heard footsteps on the gravel path. It was the police night-watch having another look at the kirks.

As it happened this was a very special night. It was the annual celebration of the marriage of Queen Victoria to the German Prince Albert eighteen years before. To mark the happy event a great ball for the gentry was being held in Dalkeith Palace by the Duke and Duchess of Buccleuch. Five hundred coaches, carrying rich and important people, from Edinburgh and round about, had gone to the ball.

In the early morning most of the guests were driven back to Edinburgh and many returned by Candlemaker Row. None of them realised that a shivering, hungry, heart-broken wee terrier was spending the night by his master's grave.

After the sound of the horses and carriages had gone, Bobby heard the clatter of hob-nailed boots as people went to work. Most of them were bakers hurrying off to bake the morning rolls.

Bobby peeped out. The rain had stopped. He thought he saw several bright stars behind the bare branches of the trees. But they were the lights of the Castle where the sentries marched to and fro on the ramparts.

Bobby waited for the morning light. Would his master rise up and take him for a walk to the coffee-house to get him a bun or a pie? Bobby licked his lips. He was very cold and hungry.

At last the sky lightened over the roofs of Candlemaker Row. From the Castle a bugle sounded 'Reveille' telling the soldiers to rise and begin their duties.

Some minutes later, about sunrise, James Brown appeared from his house nearby. He unlocked the Kirk Gate and came towards the new grave.

'Ah, that lazy Jamie Dunn,' he muttered. 'No here yet tae start a day's work!' He was in a bad mood.

Suddenly he spotted Bobby. He shouted and shook his spade at him.

'Aff ye get, ye rascal. Dugs is no allowed in the yaird. What's yer business

40

here? Hoo did ye get in? Wha let ye in?'

In answer to all these questions Bobby merely growled and showed his teeth, sharp and business-like. He was a fighting dog. He refused to budge from his master's grave for this bad-tempered old man.

The gardener lifted his spade to threaten Bobby but Bobby ran behind him and snapped at his ankles. To avoid being bitten, the old man stepped up on the lower table-stone out of reach of Bobby's teeth. But Bobby was jumping with rage so the gardener crossed over to the higher table-stone. Even there he didn't feel secure.

At that moment, James Dunn arrived to fill in the grave. He laughed at the sight of the gardener besieged by a small terrier. This only made James Brown angrier.

'Man,' said Dunn, 'are ye blin? That's Auld Jock's wee Bobby. D'ye no mind he was at the burial yestreen?'

'Michty me! Bless my soul! Sae he is,' said James Brown. 'I'm fair ashamed o mysel for no kennin him. The puir bit beastie has come back tae the yaird tae lie aside his deid maister. I'll awa back tae the hoose and bring him a bite o breakfast.' He hurried away and soon Bobby was enjoying a bowl of porridge and milk, all angry feelings now subdued.

In the forenoon Young Jock called at the burial office near the kirk gate to pay his father's burial charges. On the previous day he had taken the responsibility of registering his father's death with Mr Laing the St Giles district registrar and signing his name in the book.

He now paid over the money for the burial expenses. The grave-digging cost three shillings; turf to cover the grave four shillings; registration cost three shillings; the certificate of burial signed by John Raeburn one shilling. The dearest item was the mort-cloth, but nobody grudged the five shilling fee as it was given to charity.

Having satisfied the burial officer, Young Jock tried to grab Bobby to take him home but Bobby knew very well what he intended to do and dodged his grasp, refusing to leave the grave, so no further attempt was made that day to remove him.

After that first cold morning, there was a fine spell of weather. The wind was light and the sun shone from eight in the morning until five in the afternoon. Each day became a little longer. Spring was slowly on the way, as thrushes and blackbirds sang cheerily from the trees and the gables of the combined kirks.

The nights were certainly cold and moonless for some time but Bobby didn't worry. He was being given food and water by James Brown, who also laid a sack under the table-stone for him to lie on. He wanted to show Bobby that he was sorry for not recognising him on that first cold morning.

The night-policemen heard about Bobby and shone their lanterns on him as he lay under his great stone roof. They remembered him as John Gray's watch-dog and gave him a bit of their 'piece'.

Ancient gravestones against the houses of Candlemaker Row.

Several of the houses in Candlemaker Row had back windows looking across to the kirkyard where Bobby wandered about. In number 28 Candlemaker Row, at the back, above the public house now known as Greyfriars Bobby Bar, lived and worked James Anderson, an upholsterer. His skill as a craftsman was much in demand. He had been in the house for several years but in all that time he had never seen a dog running free in the burial-yard though it was notorious for the great number of cats of all sizes and colours that roamed there. Nobody had yet invented a gate to keep out cats.

Robert Louis Stevenson, a frequent visitor to Greyfriars during Bobby's vigil there, wrote that he had seen as many as thirteen cats stretched out on the grave of a famous judge. As this was the same unlucky number that made a full meeting of witches, Stevenson had an idea that perhaps it was a meeting of witches, who had changed themselves into cats, and were feasting on strange and horrible meats in Greyfriars.

So, although James Anderson was not surprised to see cats, he was puzzled at the rare sight of a dog. He was even more puzzled because James Brown was allowing it to stay, when it was one of his paid duties to keep dogs and children out of Greyfriars. He was even feeding it, and providing it with a warm bed!

Anderson soon found out Bobby's identity and on stormy nights he went down to the table-stone and coaxed him out. He took him out by the Kirk Gate, with Brown's permission, and gave him a warm bed by the fire at number 28.

By the time early summer arrived, with blossoming trees and sweet scented flowers in the kirkyard, Bobby had settled into his new life. He had made many friends and some good folk were caring for him. He still wondered about his master's disappearance but he knew he was nearby and it was sufficient just to know he was close to him.

42

Bobbby and the One O'clock Gun.

When Mrs Gray and Young Jock visited the grave, they tried to persuade Bobby to come home with them. If they simply carried him home, he howled and scratched at the door until they let him out, when he trotted back to the kirkyard.

But the Grays did not stay long at Hall's Court. Their house belonged to the police and seven weeks after her husband's death Mrs Gray was asked to vacate it. She was delighted to leave Hall's Court since the police had provided her with another house in a better district. How long she and Young Jock lived in Edinburgh is not known but probably they returned to the country, for neither of them remained in the St Giles district or were buried beside Auld Jock because their names are not to be found in the Greyfriars Burial Record.

However faithful he was to his master, Bobby was wise to the ways of the world. Given the chance of a bed and a supper in James Anderson's house or later that year in the house of Robert Ritchie the tailor and his daughter, also in number 28, he left the cold of the kirkyard for as long as the weather proved unpleasant, never failing to return to his earthen bed when the skies cleared.

He often visited Mr and Mrs Ramsay's Eating House where he used to go with Auld Jock, and he was always sure of a warm welcome and a bite to eat.

Throughout the year there were memorable days in Edinburgh but perhaps the most enjoyable for all concerned was Queen Victoria's birthday, celebrated on 24th of May. For weeks beforehand children sang this defiant verse.

> The twenty-fourth of May
> Is the Queen's birthday
> If you don't give us a holiday
> We'll all run away.

The schools were closed that day as the authorities had to show their loyalty. But if they had remained open very few children would have attended. They would have played truant or 'kipped the schule' as they always did when a circus came to town or anything exciting occurred.

Around nine o'clock in the evening, after sunset, bonfires lit up the whole town. The biggest was on the summit of Arthur's Seat, the extinct volcano that has all the rugged features of a great mountain though it is only 823ft. high. But every street in the thickly populated parts of the city had a huge bonfire and for weeks before the great day, gangs of youngsters raided

43

neighbouring streets, stealing their stores of bonfire wood.

Fireworks were set off by the thousand, as gunpowder was cheap and plentiful. Everybody could afford squibs, small explosive fireworks; but harmless sparklers, catherine wheels and coloured matches were preferred by the girls, who left the older boys and men to let off 'cannons' or to fire rockets high above the roof tops.

Boys and girls had a glorious time, the more adventurous trying to jump over the bonfires and often singeing their clothes. But for dogs, cats and horses it was a terrifying experience, though luckily most horses were safe in their stables before sunset.

But Bobby was not easily scared. In fact, bonfires and squibs excited him and he barked and joined in the fun.

The summer passed quickly and autumn spread the kirkyard with a thick carpet of leaves. Bobby loved to frolic amongst them, and chase them as they blew in the wind.

Winter was great fun too, especially when the snow clouds came drifting over the city from the Pentland or Moorfoot Hills and Edinburgh awoke to find itself no longer dirty and sooty, a perfect, white blanket covering the Town. The Castle stood high on the rock like a great picture drawn with black ink on pure white paper.

Boys and girls were excited by the scene. The snow was reflected on the ceiling and walls and even the dingiest houses looked as if they had been spring-cleaned. The young folk could hardly eat breakfast, they were so eager to go sledging on the hills or the steep streets or battle it out in a snowball fight.

Bobby tried to plough through the drifts but was unable to make any headway with his short legs and he had to jump about from place to place. When it was frosty, he crunched his way over the hard, frozen snow quite cheerfully.

He now regarded Greyfriars as his own property, and being a fighting dog, he chased all the cats away. When the Heriot's schoolboys climbed over the dividing wall from their playground Bobby was after them like a shot, barking at their heels as they clambered back into their own ground.

In 1859 the Ramsays gave up the Eating House and left the district. Mr William Paterson took over the business. He had heard all about Bobby, so he willingly fed him each day as the Ramsays had done.

On the Queen's Birthday 24th May 1861, Mr Paterson ended his year as restaurant keeper and Mr James Currie took over the business. He also welcomed Bobby, who had now known three keepers of the Eating House.

Shortly after Mr Currie's arrival, a strange and exciting event occurred in Edinburgh. It all started with a visit to the city several years before by a sea-captain from a foreign country. When he returned home, he reported that he had just visited a wonderful city, full of splendid buildings and monuments, where wise men and lovely ladies lived, and where every science was

44

studied. There was only one problem. Nobody knew the correct time of day. In other words, there were many clocks of all kinds and the kirk clocks chimed the hours and the quarter hours. But no two clocks agreed.

To put this right, in 1853, a time-signal in the form of a large canvas-covered ball, was constructed to slide up and down the mast on the top of Nelson's Monument on the Calton Hill. Shortly before one o'clock each afternoon, the ball was hoisted to the top of the mast. Exactly at one o'clock it was lowered. Sea-captains anchored in the Firth of Forth near Leith could see the signal through their spy-glasses and put their ship's clocks right. Edinburgh people could also set the correct time.

In 1861, Bobby's fourth year in Greyfriars, the men in charge of the Royal Observatory, on the Calton Hill, decided to provide a much more accurate signal that would be heard far and near. In Paris a cannon was being fired daily at one o'clock to give the time, so Edinburgh decided to do the same.

In fact, Edinburgh decided to offer a better service by firing a cannon every hour. Luckily, this was thought to be too much of a good thing, and it was limited to one signal a day at one o'clock.

A long copper wire connected Edinburgh Castle to the Royal Observatory and Nelson's Column on the Calton Hill. An electric clock was connected to the system and hung on the wall near the Half-moon Battery of the Castle. When the second-hand arrived at exactly one o'clock, the gun was automatically discharged and the ball on Nelson's Column dropped simultaneously. There was no cannon-ball fired, of course; the gun was only loaded with gunpowder.

5th June 1861, was the day fixed for the first signal, and everybody put their fingers to their ears and waited. But one o'clock came and passed without event. The machinery had failed. On 6th June everyone covered their ears again. But once more, no bang. The machinery was blamed again.

But on 7th June, the town was startled by a sharp report. Pigeons took flight in panic. It was third time lucky.

People set their watches and clocks by the gun. For the first time Edinburgh knew the correct time and everybody felt very proud.

You may wonder what the one o'clock gun had to do with wee Bobby. Well, there is an interesting story here.

There was a Sergeant Scott of the Royal Engineers stationed at Edinburgh Castle who got to hear about Bobby in the summer of 1861. He was very fond of dogs, so naturally, when he found Bobby he made a special pet of him. Every week he brought Bobby a feed of steak, which was cooked for him in Currie's Eating House where Sergeant Scott occasionally had dinner.

Bobby was happy to go for a walk with this kind soldier, so the Sergeant took him to the Castle and introduced him to his friends. It is said that Bobby got very excited when the pipes and drums played on the parade ground.

Either the Royal Engineers or the Royal Artillery, being trained men specially appointed to Edinburgh Castle, were put in charge of priming the time-gun. Bobby, who was not afraid of big bangs, was allowed to stand close by when the gun was fired.

A very clear sketch of this daily event was drawn at the time by an artist, and printed in a popular magazine called *Good Words* which was read all over the English-speaking world.

The sketch, as you can see, shows three soldiers attending the gun. On the left is a warrant officer, his rank shown by four stripes. In the centre of the group is a sergeant and on his right a gunner. Both are wearing 'shell' uniforms, which were always worn on duty. All are wearing little round hats, known humourously as pill-boxes.

The electric clock points to one o'clock, and the gun, the muzzle pointing through the gun port, is about to fire. And there, in the bottom of the picture, as pleased as Punch, is Bobby, quite unafraid.

Sergeant Scott trained Bobby to be punctual at dinner-time. How this was done we are not quite sure, but with a clever dog like Bobby it did not take long to get him to understand that the sound of the one o'clock gun meant that dinner was ready.

Soldiers stationed in Edinburgh Castle were often very lonely as they were sometimes far from home. They were therefore very fond of making pets, usually dogs. Close by the ramparts of the Castle is the famous Dogs' Cemetery where many of these mascots' and pets' graves were marked by little tombstones. If Bobby had decided to stay with Sergeant Scott, his gravestone might have been in the Dogs' Cemetery. But his love for Auld Jock was even stronger than his love for his good soldier friend, and he always returned to Greyfriars.

It soon became a daily attraction to watch Bobby go for his dinner when he heard the one o'clock gun and a small crowd collected at the gates of the kirkyard to wait for him.

A few seconds after the cannon report, Bobby would come trotting out and head for the Eating House where he pushed open the door. James Brown must have seen to it that the gate was open daily for this very important event.

Many years later, people who witnessed this free show, wrote to the newspapers to recall how the crowds cheered Bobby as he went for his dinner. But he did not linger. As soon as he had dined he went straight back to sit by his master's grave.

Bobby never missed his one o'clock dinner. Well, hardly ever. There was one day every week which he could never understand. The restaurant was shut, and no meaty bones, pies or buns were to be had. Bobby could see no sense in this, because the kirks were open that day. Perhaps everybody went to the kirk to have something to eat, for they all seemed to be very happy and he could hear them singing and obviously enjoying themselves.

Once or twice he tried to enter the Old Greyfriars Kirk to see what was going on inside, and perhaps be lucky enough to get a bone or a bowl of steak. But the old man at the door always chased him away.

Bobby was no fool, however. On Friday and Saturday he was sometimes seen carrying bones, or scraps of food, from the Eating House, or from Mr Anderson's or Ritchie's. He took these tasty bites to the place where he lay under the table-stone, then scratched a hole and buried them.

On Sundays, when the eating-house was closed, he dug up his store and enjoyed himself, chewing away for hours.

Bobby is in Great Danger

In May 1862, John Traill with his wife, son and daughter, rented the small dwelling house at 5 Greyfriars Place and the restaurant attached to it at number 6 which had previously been kept by Mr Currie.

John Traill, aged twenty-four, was a native of Dunfermline and his wife a year younger, was born in Cupar. They were strangers to Edinburgh and were surprised and pleased to find that they had a little visitor each day just after the sound of the one o'clock gun.

They made enquiries about Bobby's owner but nobody seemed to explain the details about John Gray's death in 1858, which is very surprising as James Brown, the Greyfriars gardener was still alive (he died six years later and was buried in Greyfriars) and James Anderson and Robert Ritchie, only a few doors away, could have told them all they wanted to know about Bobby and his master.

Traill's Temperance Coffee House.

Whatever were Traill's motives, no one knows, but he began to spread a completely false story. Although he did not take over the restaurant for four and a quarter years after John Gray's death, he claimed he had entertained him in the restaurant, along with his dog. He said he was a farmer who came each day when the one o'clock gun sounded, to have his lunch. But the time-gun did not begin to fire until John Gray had been buried for nearly three and a half years, so Traill's story, repeated continuously, was obviously known by many people to be untrue. Yet he succeeded in creating a reputation for himself as the patron of Greyfriars Bobby, and was responsible for the myth of Auld Jock the farmer or shepherd of extreme old age whose home was in the Pentland Hills, which was further falsified by the American authoress Eleanor Atkinson in her book *Greyfriars Bobby*, published in 1912. The strongest evidence of the untruth of Traill's claims is in the dates on Bobby's dinner dish in Huntly House Museum, Edinburgh, which confirm he was fed by Traill from 1862-72.

Each day as the one o'clock gun fired, Bobby continued to visit the restaurant, now renamed Traill's Temperance Coffee House. And as his reputation grew, his carefully timed visits drew a crowd of curious spectators.

Bobby was now six years old, well-cared-for and full of spirits. There was no doubt he was a welcome addition to the kirkyard, normally a very sombre and tearful place. On the Sabbath the yard was crowded by worshippers attending the joint kirks in the forenoon and evening, and by visitors to the graves. The sight of a little dog guarding his master's grave appealed to the Victorians. It gave them hope that they too might be remembered after their death. It also added dignity to the graves which within living memory had been desecrated by the body-snatchers.

During weekdays, for several years after John Gray's burial, there were many other burials, as the records show. Most of these were inhabitants of the crowded closes and wynds of the parishes of St Giles and Tron. But some were residents in wealthier districts whose husbands and wives were often reunited to their dust forty or fifty years later.

Early on Sunday morning 10th November 1861, a terrible accident, which had been waiting to happen for years, convulsed not only the City of Edinburgh, but the whole English-speaking world and beyond. For months, the people living in a large 'land' or tenement on the north side of the High Street had heard creaks and cracks in the floors and walls. It was a very tall structure of about ten storeys and had been built in the reign of Charles II about 1670. Some people left in fear, but most stayed on, probably having no other retreat from the winter weather.

At one o'clock in the morning, the whole building fell with a mighty roar like thunder, throwing slates, stones, chimneys, furniture and the occupants in a great heap into the High Street. Thirty-five people were immediately crushed to death and many more were injured. One long remembered deed of heroism or rather stoicism brightened the awful scene. A young man trapped beneath a heavy beam cried out to his rescuers, 'Heave awa lads, I'm no deid yet.' He was rescued and survived for several years.

The whole town was awakened by the crash and certainly with his keen hearing, Bobby would hear it only half-a-mile away. It meant nothing to him, nor did he associate it with six funeral processions attended simultaneously by a host of weeping mourners a few days later, of victims old and young, hurled to an unexpected death.

Robert Louis Stevenson was only a schoolboy when he saw the ruin the following day. Here is his memory of it.

'The church bells never sounded more dismally over Edinburgh than that grey afternoon. None who saw it can have forgotten the aspect of the gable; here it was plastered, there papered; here a kettle still stood on the hob, high overhead; and there a cheap picture of the Queen was pasted over a chimney . . . All over the world, in London, in Canada, in New Zealand, fancy what a multitude of people could exclaim with truth, 'The house that I was born in fell last night'.

But from that time onwards, burials in Greyfriars grew less numerous and the church authorities decided to make the yard more attractive to the public by opening the gates on Sunday afternoons. Boys and girls looked forward to seeing Bobby. They were not interested in the hundreds of great tombs and sculptures all round the walls. They would rather pat Bobby and give him peppermint drops and other sweets to crunch.

The five years that Bobby had kept watch brought many changes. Old John Haywood had died a few weeks after John Gray. William Wilson, the graveman from St Cuthberts, had got his job. James Dunn who helped to bury John Gray, had retired, as had James Campbell the burial recorder.

New cemeteries such as Warriston and the Grange had been opened on the outskirts of the city and they were preferred to the over-crowded Greyfriars which had been the last resting place of many famous Scots for three hundred years.

In those days hundreds of stray and starving dogs roamed the streets of Edinburgh. In summer, owing to heat and thirst and ill-treatment, some of these poor beasts took a disease called distemper and ran about snapping at everyone. The town councillors ordered that all dogs were to be muzzled, but this was not easily done and it caused the dogs much hardship.

The duty, or licence, on every dog kept in Scotland had been twelve shillings (sixty pence), a large sum then. Few people paid it, so it was reduced to seven shillings (thirty-five pence) for the first licence and only five shillings (twenty-five pence) each year afterwards. A licence was not required for puppies under six months or working-dogs and watch-dogs.

Anyone disobeying this law was fined £5. If a dog was seen in a house, that was enough to establish it as the property of the householder.

One April morning Bobby heard a hammering on the kirk door. He trotted round to see what was going on. A policeman was nailing a paper to the door. Bobby went back to his shelter as he did not think it had anything to do with him. But it had. It was a notice telling everybody where and when dog-licences were to be paid.

A day or two later two policemen called at Traill's Coffee House.

'Whaur's yer dog, Mr. Traill?' they asked.

'I dinna hae a dog, officer,' Mr. Traill replied.

'Come awa noo. Dinna try tae get oot o it. A dog's been seen coming here every day at one o'clock. Ye feed him. Dinna tell us it's no your dog.'

'It's certainly no my dog. It's John Gray's dog. Everybody kens that,' said Mr. Traill.

The policemen laughed. 'Aye, and everybody kens John Gray's been deid for mony a year. Ye dinna expect him tae pey the licence, dae ye?'

'I dinna intend tae pay, wha ever does,' said Traill.

'A' richt, dinna pey,' said the policeman. 'Ye'll get a summons tae appear in the Burgh Court. Maybe ye'll see reason then.'

That same day, James Brown got to hear about the threat to Bobby. He was very upset for he had loved Bobby ever since that first cold morning

Bobby with the Traill family.

51

Auld Jock's grave and the two table-stones.

when he had tried to chase him away.

'John,' he said to Traill, 'I've very little money but I'll spare some tae save wee Bobby.'

Next day John Traill received a summons to appear in court on 12th April.

In court he explained all about Bobby, whom he had known for four years. The other people, who had known him longer, could back up his story. The case was dismissed, but Bobby still had no owner and was likely to be destroyed. He did not know he was in danger and was happy as ever, running for his dinner at the sound of the gun.

Most of the police were kind-hearted men, but they had to obey orders.

Here is how the dog-catchers used to work. A driver and two policemen came round with the dog-wagon. When they saw a stray dog, one man caught it with a catch-pole with iron hoops that tightened round its neck. The second policeman threw a sack over the dog's head to stop it from biting him. It was then put into a wagon and driven away with the other strays to be poisoned.

Was Bobby to be treated like this, after all these years of watching by his master's grave?

James Anderson and Robert Ritchie decided to take Bobby up to the City Chambers to pay for his licence.

Now the Lord Provost of Edinburgh was William Chambers, a famous

Lord Provost, Sir William Chambers.

book publisher and a director of the Scottish Society for the Prevention of Cruelty to Animals. He was a lover of dogs.

When Provost Chambers heard about Bobby he asked the City Officer, Mr MacPherson, to bring Bobby along to his house. The Provost was so delighted with Bobby that he promised to pay his licence for as long as he lived. He argued that, as the Town Council owned Greyfriars Burial Ground and encouraged the dog to stay there, they were the owners. He himself, as head of the Town Council, had a duty to pay his licence.

Provost Chambers kept his word. He also had a collar made for Bobby with a brass plate on it with the following inscription: 'Greyfriars Bobby from the Lord Provost, 1867, licensed'.

Bobby was now safe. Little did he realise his narrow escape from death.

Now the strange thing about this attempt to destroy Bobby is that his fidelity to his master had become well known throughout Scotland and perhaps further afield three years before the fuss about his licence.

The *Inverness Courier* of 10th May 1864 published a story about a little terrier named Bob. It gives all the details about him lying under the shelter of an old pillared tombstone, about him taking an occasional night's lodgings with some of his acquaintances and of him coming out of the Greyfriars Kirkyard to get a biscuit or a sandwich from the publican or the baker. It also mentions his friendship with Sergeant Scott of the Royal Engineers, one of the team seconded to fire the one o'clock gun.

But the article is in error when the writer states, 'No one knows whose death he mourns or where he comes from although the general feeling is that

53

he came from the country with a funeral cortege.' It is also wrong when it states that Bobby did not accompany Scott beyond the end of George 1V Bridge.

So even as early as 1864, the story, though not accurate, was widely publicised, as other newspapers copied it from the *Inverness Courier*. Apparently nobody thought of asking James Brown (who did not die until 1868) or James Anderson or Robert Ritchie, about the owner of the dog, John Gray; nobody thought of consulting the Mortality Recorder; of visiting Register House to inspect John Gray's Death Certificate or of calling at the Police Office to consult the records. Neither did anyone know what the Church Officer could have told them, that a country cortege, or for that matter any old shepherd or farmer from outwith the city, could not obtain burial in the High Yard of Greyfriars.

An even stranger aspect of the above article is the 'confession' made in the autobiography of T Wilson Reid, an Ayr journalist, that he wrote the article of 1864 and that he made the whole story up as he was short of copy. But most of the details of his story are too circumstantial to support his 'confession', and furthermore, there are reliable witnesses supported by the Valuation Rolls to verify that Bobby was present at the grave of John Gray from early 1858 onwards.

The whole incident is very odd even at the distance of one hundred and twenty years. Why should anyone wish to destroy a dog that had been universally admired for several years? Why did John Traill refuse to part with seven shillings to save a dog that was bringing him profit and publicity and to which his family was fondly attached? Why did Lord Provost Sir William Chambers receive so much praise for his expenditure of a few shillings when he was finally responsible for the presence of the dog in the Burial Ground owned by the City? He was also President of the Scottish Society for the Prevention of Cruelty to Animals!

There appears to have been no lack of hypocrisy in mid-Victorian Edinburgh. The whole incident emphasises human perfidy against a notable background of canine honesty and fidelity and supports Madame Roland's celebrated dictum, 'The more I see of men, the more I love dogs'.

Bobby is now Famous

Although Bobby was well known to a few people in the Greyfriars district after the death of his master, he did not really attract attention until he started his daily dinner routine at the sound of the one o'clock gun.

Following his narrow escape from the dog-catchers, and the Lord Provost's payment of his licence and gift of a collar, his story was reported in many newspapers and he became famous throughout the country.

Artists came to Greyfriars Kirkyard and sketched and painted him, and people took his photograph.

As word spread, offers of support came from lovers of animals all over Britain and the niece of a famous English writer offered to send Bobby a comfortable kennel.

If Bobby had been a human being he might have become proud and conceited, but, being a wee Skye terrier, his life went on as usual. He asked no more than his daily dinner at Mr Traill's, or an occasional bed or meal from Mr Anderson, Mr Ritchie or his daughter Maria, a straw-bonnet maker, who kept house for her widowed father.

The memorial drinking fountain and Greyfriars Bobby Bar.

Bobby, dog-like, was always attached to anyone who fed him. He is also known to have paid regular visits over several years to the public-house at the head of Candlemaker Row, now named Greyfriars Bobby Bar.

There was another licensed house in the Bristo district close by, called The Hole i' the Wa' which Bobby also visited. It stood in a gap in the great Flodden Wall, built in 1513-14 and strengthened in 1544 on threat of another English invasion. The residents of Brown Square near this pub long remembered Bobby.

Mr Dow, a joiner in Heriot's School, was also Bobby's friend. Bobby waited each day as Mr Dow took a short cut through the graveyard to Traill's restaurant. If Mr Dow did not appear, Bobby went alone, as he was usually hungry.

Mr Dow died in 1871 and Bobby was puzzled, as he couldn't understand such disappearances.

In November 1871, some people talked about erecting a monument to Bobby, but as he was still alive, nothing was done about it.

Bobby was now sixteen. Some terriers have been known to live longer, but not many. To have reached such an age means that he did not lie out in all weathers. That would have soon killed him. Even lying on a blanket under the table-stone was very weakening in cold weather. No doubt his friends who fed and sheltered him, lengthened his life by many years.

It appears John Traill and his family adopted Bobby and looked after him for some time before his death. Elizabeth Traill used to take Bobby out for walks. She stated, years after his death, that she was always glad to return home as he tried to pick a quarrel with every male dog he met.

In the last year of Bobby's life, and perhaps a year or two before, Traill employed two girls, Anne Mackay and Agnes Cunningham, both natives of Lanarkshire, to help in the Temperance Coffee Shop. The meagre accommodation at numbers 5 and 6 was taxed to the full and these 'skivvies' probably shared a box-bed. It is quite likely that these girls exercised Bobby and like him, looked forward to a spell of fresh air and some company.

By the beginning of the year Bobby was weak from old age and on Sunday evening 14th January 1872, he fell asleep by the fireside and didn't waken.

Mr Traill and a few friends secretly buried Bobby in a triangular flower plot beneath a tree, in front of Old Greyfriars Kirk. They did not dare bury him beside Auld Jock on consecrated ground, although Bobby had mourned for his master much more sincerely than many Christians would have done for their friends.

A stone carved with the words 'Greyfriars Bobby' was put over his grave, but it was soon removed by a Burial Officer. James Brown cannot be blamed for this, as Bobby's friend, the gardener, died on 24th March 1868.

Nobody now knows the exact spot where Bobby lies at the front of the Kirk, but he is near Auld Jock and, in life, that was always his greatest concern.

Many things connected with Bobby can still be seen today. The most famous of these, of course, is his monument at the top of Candlemaker Row, donated to the city by Baroness Angela Georgina Burdett-Coutts.

The Baroness heard about Bobby shortly before he died and being an animal lover, offered to erect a memorial fountain to keep his memory alive after his death. The town council of the City of Edinburgh gratefully accepted her offer.

The fountain was of red granite, with drinking-water provided for the public and a trough at the bottom for dogs. On top of the fountain was placed a life-size bronze model of Bobby, made by the famous sculptor, William Brodie R.S.A. The statue was unveiled on 15th November 1873, and Baroness Burdett-Coutts was honoured by being given the freedom of Edinburgh.

The plaque on the memorial fountain reads as follows:

A tribute to the affectionate fidelity of Greyfriars Bobby. In 1858 this faithful dog followed the remains of his master to Greyfriars Churchyard and lingered near the spot until his death in 1872. With permission erected by Baroness Burdett-Coutts.

A number of American visitors to Greyfriars, who had read about Bobby at school in America, collected money to erect a gravestone, also in red granite, to his memory, in the Kirkyard. As a dog's grave was not allowed there, the stone was erected as a memorial to John Gray over his grave and Bobby was mentioned on it. It reads as follows:

JOHN GRAY

DIED 1858

'AULD JOCK'

MASTER OF 'GREYFRIARS BOBBY'

'AND EVEN IN HIS ASHES MOST BELOVED'

ERECTED BY

AMERICAN LOVERS OF 'BOBBY'

In 1981 the Dog Aid Society of Scotland presented and erected a red granite memorial to Bobby similar to the stone at Auld Jock's grave. The memorial grave-stone was unveiled by the Duke of Gloucester and there was a service with a children's choir.

This memorial is not on consecrated ground but on the triangular grass plot in front of the Kirk where reliable witnesses, including Bailie Wilson MacLaren testified that Bobby was buried.

Two of Bobby's own things are still to be seen in Huntly House Museum in the Canongate of Edinburgh. One is the collar presented to him in 1867 by Lord Provost Sir William Chambers. The other is his metal dinner dish which a grand-daughter of John Traill gave to the city. Bobby fed from it in the Coffee Shop from May 1862 until January 1872, just before he died. On it is engraved 'Bobby's Dinner Dish'.

In the same case as these articles there are photographs of John Traill, and of Bobby seated between Elizabeth and her brother, Alexander. Elizabeth is dressed in a long, checked frock and Alexander wears a kilt and jacket. There are also photographs of John Traill and his family with Bobby, and a view of Traill's Temperance Coffee House.

Bobby's collar and dinner dish.

Other articles include the plaster cast of Bobby from which William Brodie made the bronze statue.

Not far away is Dr Littlejohn's Baton of Office, given to him when he was made Edinburgh's first Medical Officer of Health, four years after he attended John Gray, though no one has ever suspected until now that he had a close connection with Bobby.

If you are in Edinburgh you should pay a visit to Huntly House Museum and see these things.

So here ends the story of Greyfriars Bobby, the wee Skye terrier, who, like all great heroes in the world, was not afraid of danger and the dreadful people and places he lived amongst. The love of his master kept him steadfast during bad weather, hunger, and the threat of death.

St Francis must be proud to have such a faithful creature as Greyfriars Bobby asleep forever in his garden.

Press Reports and Eye-witness Accounts.

The Scotsman, 18 April 1867.

Since the story of this dog was told in *The Scotsman* a few days ago, the animal has become an object of much interest and many persons have gone to see it in its home among the tombs. Mr Gourlay Steell, R.S.A., is already far advanced with a picture in tempera, showing the faithful sentinel on the grave of his late master... While sitting for his portrait in Mr Steell's studio, Bobby, on hearing the report of the time-gun—his usual call to dinner—got quite excited, and refused to be pacified until supplied with his mid-day meal. The picture, we understand, will be on view next week in Mr Clark's Art Gallery, Princes Street.

Staff Reporter.

The Scotsman, 17 January 1872.

GREYFRIARS' BOBBY: Many will be sorry to hear that the poor but interesting dog, 'Greyfriars' Bobby', died on Sunday evening. Every kind attention was paid to him in his last days by his guardian, Mr Traill, who has had him buried in a flower-plot near Greyfriars' church. His collar, a gift from Lord Provost Chambers, has been deposited in the office at the church gate. Mr Brodie, we understand, has successfully modelled the figure of Greyfriars' Bobby, which is to surmount the very handsome memorial to be erected by the munificence of the Baroness Burdett-Coutts.

Staff Reporter.

The Scotsman, 2 August 1934.

When at George Watson's School in 1870 I used to get my dinner at Traill's Eating House near the Greyfriars Churchyard, and every day a little dog came in for his bite from the kind-hearted Mr Traill. This would likely be Bobby, and if so he must have survived his old master quite a number of years.

William Albert Cunningham
40 Leamington Terr.
Edinburgh.

The Scotsman, 2 August 1934.

As an old Edinburgh citizen I have been greatly interested in the recent references to Greyfriars' Bobby, culminating in your excellent article today.

In 1868 and 1869 I often had the pleasure of seeing Bobby leaving the churchyard to get his dinner. The scene was, of course, a daily occurrence. Towards one o'clock people would gather just outside the large entrance gates, forming a line on each side of the sloping causeway. So widespread was the interest that every class of society was represented, from the well-to-do and fashionably dressed to the artisan and the humble message-boy. As the hour drew near there was a hush of expectation. Then bang went the gun in the Castle, and every head turned to the gate, knowing that at the signal Bobby would break his lonely vigil and set off on the way out. Soon there was a hushed whisper, 'Here he comes!' and the grey, shaggy little figure appeared, pattering over the causeway between the two lines of people. Looking neither to one side nor the other, intent only on his own affairs, Bobby hurried round the corner to his right, up the street a few yards, and disappeared into Mr Traill's Dining Rooms for the meal he never failed to get for many years.

By those who cared to wait long enough, his return could also be seen. His dinner finished in reasonable time, the devoted dog, with no interval for idle frolics, returned once more to the grave of his master.

Andrew Hislop, Edinburgh.

The Scotsman, 13 August 1934.

. . . Who does not know the monument to Gray? But the dog's dust is not there. Some thirty years ago a friend of my own—Session-Clerk to one of the Greyfriars Churches—pointed at the centre of the triangular piece of ground between the gate-way and the older Church as the spot at which Bobby was buried.

R T Skinner, Edinburgh.

The Scotsman, 16 August 1934.

It may interest many readers of *The Scotsman* to know that at one time, on the triangular bit of ground facing the entrance to Greyfriars Kirkyard, a stone was surreptitiously placed where Bobby was buried. The kindly John

Traill, and a few other admirers of the dog, procured a small stone, and had the words 'Greyfriars Bobby' roughly chiselled out. One night, I, along with the others, crept out of the coffee-house back window, which looked into the kirkyard. A tree stood near the spot at that time, but is now removed. Quickly a hole was dug, and the stone placed in position. There it remained for several months; then, presumably acting on orders, the curator of the burial ground had it taken away.

A photograph of Bobby's resting-place, with the stone, was taken by a friend of Mr Traill's. Much to my regret, at the moment I cannot lay my hands on it. It would be an interesting 'side-light', showing a few young men's appreciation of a dog whose wonderful devotion to its dead master is known throughout the whole of the civilised world.

(Councillor) Wilson McLaren, Edinburgh.

The Scotsman, 5 March 1953.

I was interested to read the letter about 'Greyfriars Bobby' because, when I was a little girl, I stroked Bobby and held the little dog in my arms many times.

My father, William Dow, was a joiner and cabinetmaker at George Heriot's Hospital, and, in connection with his business, frequently used the private path leading from the school grounds to the Churchyard gate.

One day, about one o'clock, when my father was on his way to visit his friend Mr Traill, the little dog ran to him at the gate and followed him to the coffee-house in Greyfriars Place, where he was given a meal. That would be in 1858 or 1859.

Regularly every day afterwards, when the one o'clock gun was fired at the Castle, Bobby was there at the gate. If my father failed to appear, the little dog went on its way alone to Mr Traill's, where a good meal awaited it.

I have recollections of accompanying my father, with Bobby, to the coffee-house on several occasions. I remember Mr Traill well—a very nice and kind man.

My father was devoted to Bobby for many years, and we tried repeatedly to coax the little dog to our home, but it would not leave the Churchyard except to visit the coffee-house.

My father died in 1871—shortly after we moved to Murrayfield. The next year, my mother, wondering about Bobby, sent me to the Churchyard, but, much to my disappointment, the little dog was nowhere to be seen, so it was with great interest that I read of the burial of Bobby.

Mrs H Meldrum, Joppa, Edinburgh.